if

To Adrian and Sebastian and all future men.
—C. R. S. Jr.

Atheneum Books for Young Readers • An imprint of Simon & Schuster Children's Publishing Division • 1230 Avenue of the Americas
New York, New York 10020 • Photographs copyright © 2007 by Charles R. Smith Jr. • All rights reserved, including the right of
reproduction in whole or in part in any form. • Book design by Sonia Chaghatzbanian • The text for this book is set in Triplex. • The
illustrations for this book are photographs. • Manufactured in China • 0611 SCP • 10 9 8 7 6 5 4 3 2 • Library of Congress Cataloging-
in-Publication Data • Kipling, Rudyard, 1865–1936. • If / Rudyard Kipling ; illustrated by Charles R. Smith Jr.—1st ed. • p. cm. •
ISBN-13: 978-0-689-87799-5 • ISBN-10: 0-689-87799-4 • I. Smith Jr., Charles R., ill. II. Title. • PR4854.I4 2006 • 821'.8—dc22 • 2006005312

RUDYARD
KIPLING

if

PHOTOGRAPHS BY CHARLES R. SMITH JR.

atheneum books for young readers · new york london toronto sydney

ginee seo books

a father's advice to his son

If you can keep your head when all about you

Are losing theirs
and blaming it on you,

If you can trust yourself

when all men doubt you,

But make allowance for their doubting too;

If
you can wait
and not be tired by waiting,

Or being lied about,
don't deal in lies,

Or being hated, don't give way to hating,

And yet don't look too good, nor talk too wise:

If
you can dream—

and not make
dreams your
master;

If
you can
think—

and not make thoughts your aim;

If you can meet with Triumph and Disaster

And treat those two impostors just the same;

If

**you can bear
to hear the truth
you've spoken**

Twisted by knaves to
make a trap for fools,

**Or watch the things
you gave your life to, broken,**

**And stoop
and build 'em up
with worn-out tools:**

If

**you can make
one heap
of all your winnings**

And risk it
on one turn of pitch-and-toss,

And lose, and start again
at your beginnings

**And never breathe a word
about your loss;**

If you can force
your heart and nerve and sinew

**To serve your turn
long after they are gone,**

And so hold on
when there is nothing in you

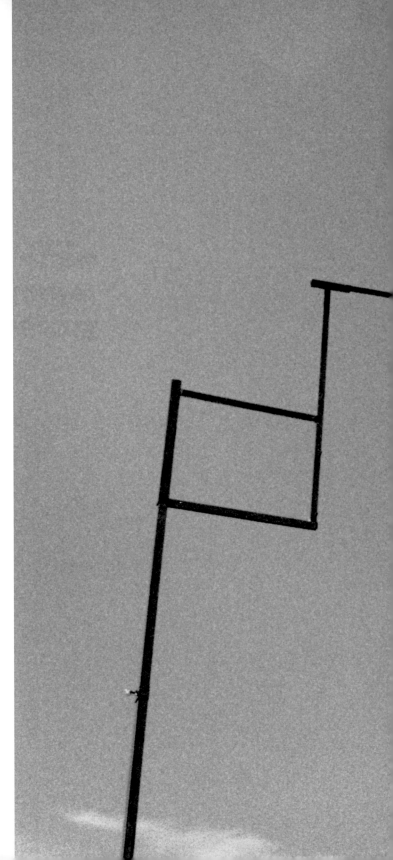

Except the Will which says to them: "Hold on!"

If you can talk with crowds and keep your virtue,

Or walk with Kings—nor lose the common touch,

If neither foes nor loving friends can hurt you,

If all men
count with you,

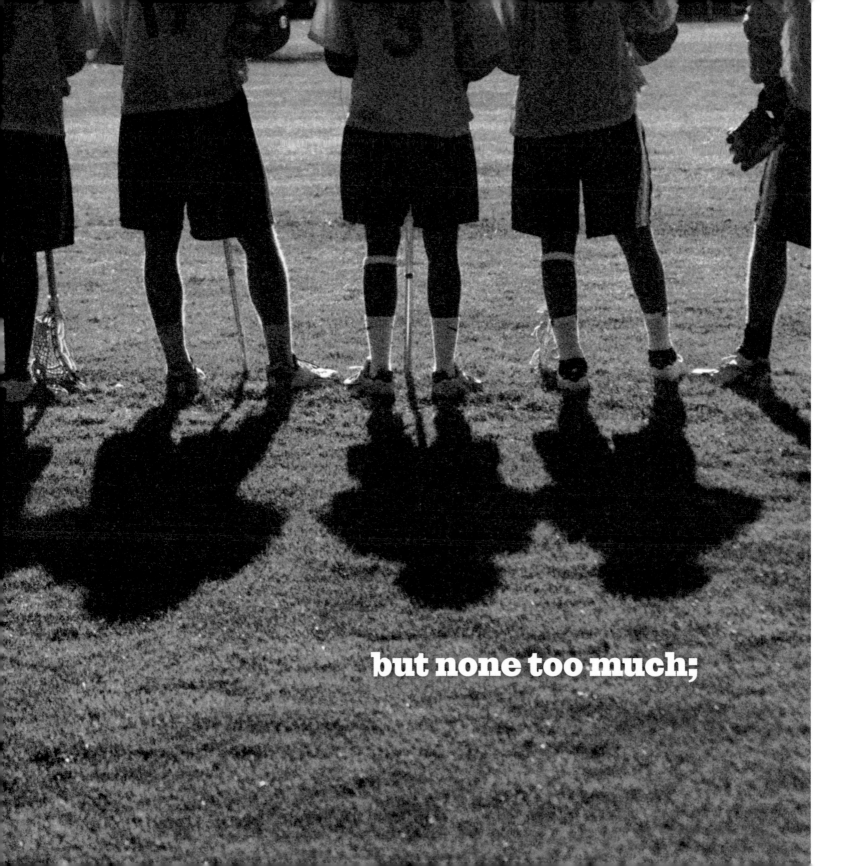

but none too much;

If you can fill
the unforgiving minute

**With sixty seconds'
worth of distance run,**

Yours
is the Earth

and everything
that's in it,

And—which is more—
you'll be a Man,
my son!

Why "If"

Back in sixth grade in Marian Anderson Elementary in Compton, California, we had to memorize a poem for an assignment. This was our first time committing a poem to memory, and the poem had to be longer than anything we had done up to that point. Our teacher gave us a list of poems to choose from and let us read all of them before we made our decision. "If" was the longest poem on the list, and if you memorized it, you got an A. Only one student in our class was able to memorize it, and no, it wasn't me. I don't remember what poem I did memorize, but I do remember enjoying "If," particularly when my classmate "performed" it to thunderous applause.

As time passed from sixth grade to junior high, to high school, to college, to my profession, I always remembered "If" and made sure I had it in my collection of poetry books. One night, searching through my books for inspiration, I came across the poem. I had just finished a great day of photographing summer basketball games, and as I read the words the images that I just snapped popped back into my head, bringing the words to life. Suddenly "If" made sense in a way that I was able to see and not just read. I was inspired by what sports have given me in my life and how the poem reflected that. This revelation led me to share this inspiring poem with others. Deciding to photograph a number of sports was easy, because all sports share the virtues explored in "If": confidence, determination, leadership, effort, and the ability to dream, among others.

And what of the author who penned this immortal poem, Mr. Rudyard Kipling? Did you know he was the same guy who wrote *The Jungle Book*? The same *Jungle Book* that later became an animated movie? He was. But don't let that fool you. Rudyard Kipling (1865—1936) was a complex man. Born to an affluent family in India, but raised for a period of time in England, he loved India for its range of people, but believed in British rule of the country and considered Indians his inferiors. At the same time he viewed authority as "blind and gross and cruel" and said it can "torment children." Many of his writings, which included poetry, short stories, and novels, reflected his racial prejudice and views on authority; many, but not all.

Personally I don't care about Rudyard Kipling's life as much as I do the work he left behind, particularly this poem. It's often difficult to separate the artist from his art, but art is pure expression, driven by everything the artist deals with in his life, including the period of time in which it is created. Times change, but how we view art stays the same. If it affects us in some way emotionally, then the artist has done his job.

In these poetic words, I have been inspired to create a work of art that I hope inspires you.

—*Charles R. Smith Jr.*